CHANGING TIMES

School

Ruth Thomson

Watts Books
London • New York • Sydney

Note for parents and teachers

The Changing Times series is soundly based on the requirements of the History Curriculum. Using the device of four generations of a real family, the author combines reminiscences of this family with other people's oral evidence. The oral history is matched with photographs and other contemporary sources. Many other lessons are hidden in the text, which practises the skills of chronological sequencing, gives reference to a timeline and introduces the language and vocabulary of the past. Young children will find much useful information here, as well as a new understanding of the recent history of everyday situations and familiar things.

© Watts Books 1994

Paperback edition 1995

Watts Books
96 Leonard Street
London
EC2A 4RH

Franklin Watts Australia
14 Mars Road
Lane Cove
NSW 2066

UK ISBN: 0 7496 1488 9 (hardback)
UK ISBN: 0 7496 1814 0 (paperback)

Dewey Decimal Classification Number 371

A CIP catalogue record for this book is available from the British Library.

Editor: Sarah Ridley
Designer: Michael Leaman
Photographer: Peter Millard
Picture researcher: Sarah Moule

The author and publisher would like to thank the following people for their help in the preparation of this book: Debbie, Emma, Andrew, Ron, Gwen and Tom Hallam, Fiona Dodwell, Malcolm Leeke, Suzanne Toleman and children from Market Deeping County Primary School.

Printed in Malaysia

Contents

My name is Emma.
I was born in 1986.
I have one sister, called Amy.
She is younger than me.

My name is Andrew.
I am Emma's father.
I was born in 1957.

My name is Ronald.
I am Andrew's father
and Emma's grandfather.
I was born in 1934.

My name is Thomas.
I am Ronald's father,
Andrew's grandfather
and Emma's great-grandfather.
I was born in 1905.

This is my school.
It is in our town.
Mum drives me here
every day.

There are 24 children
in my class.
The girls wear
grey tunics or skirts.
The boys wear grey trousers.
Our sweatshirts have the name of the school on them.

We do maths every day.

We practise
making shapes.

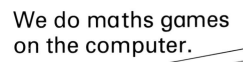

We learn about money.

We do maths games
on the computer.

We use calculators
to work out big sums.

We can choose our own reading books.
We take them home at night,
so our mums and dads
can listen to us.

We practise
joined-up writing
in our workbooks.

We are learning
about the Earth.
We find out
about rocks.

Our teacher has read us a story about monsters.

We paint pictures
and make models
of them.

There is a pond
in the school grounds.
In springtime, we dip nets
and jam jars into the water
to see what lives there.

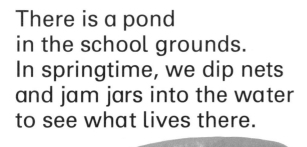

The school has
a big playground.
We play tag and football.

We can skip, catch ball or play chess.

We do gym and
dancing in the hall.

Once a week,
we go swimming.

I asked Dad whether school was the same when he was young.

He said,

'I went to the village school.
It was so near, I could walk there by myself.
A lollipop man stood outside to see us safely across the road.'

'We sat in pairs at desks
with lids that lifted up.
The desks were in rows
facing the teacher.'

Run, little dog, run.
Look at the little dog.
The little dog can run fast.

The little dog can jump.
Jump, little dog, jump.
Mother, look at my little dog.

10   11

'We learned to read
with Janet and John books.'

'There was a pretend shop
in the classroom.
We learned a lot of maths
by buying, weighing
and selling things there.'

I asked Dad about other lessons.

He said,

'We did gym in the hall.
We wore shorts
and vests.'

'A lady came to teach us crafts.
We made raffia mats,
calendars and pots out of clay.'

'Once a week, we listened
to music on the radio.
A presenter told us what to do.
We had to pretend to be trees
or fierce animals.'

'In my last year, a swimming pool
was built in the playground.
I learnt to swim in it.'

County of Lincoln — Parts of Kesteven
Education Committee

First Proficiency
Swimming Certificate

1. Dive from the Side *Sitting* fair standard
2. First Stroke *Breast-Stroke* good standard
3. Second Stroke *Back Crawl* fair standard

Awarded to

Andrew Hallam
Branston C.E. Controlled Primary School
in the 19*68* Swimming Season

A.S. Kemp
Head Teacher

F.W.C. Jolley
Director of Education

PURLEY POOLS

SWIMMING CERTIFICATE

AWARDED TO *Andrew Hallam.*   AGE

OF THE *Branston   CE Controlled* SCHOOL

WHO CAN NOW SWIM *1 Length (11 yds)* OF THE SCHOOL POOL

crawl

A.S. Kemp HEADMASTER

21st June 19*68*   *M.J. Smith* TEACHER

I asked Dad about playtime and special days.

He said,

'The boys played football
or raced cars downhill.
In the autumn we played
conkers.'

'The girls skipped, played games
and threw balls against the wall.'

'On May Day, we put up a maypole
in the playground and danced round it.'

'Once a year, there was a school fete.
Everyone came in fancy dress.
I went as an England footballer,
the year that England won
the World Cup.'

'When Man landed on the Moon,
the whole school watched it on TV.
The headmaster told us
it was an important day in history.'

15

I asked Grandad about his school days.

He said,

'I went to the same school
as your dad.
There were only four classes
and the toilets were outside.'

'I started school when the Second World War
between England and Germany broke out.'

'We were all given gas masks
in case there was a gas attack.
We practised wearing them,
but we never needed them
for real.'

'Children were sent from big towns to live in our village.
They came to our school.
They told us that their schools had been closed
in case of bombs.'

LEAVE THIS TO US SONNY — YOU OUGHT TO BE OUT OF LONDON

MINISTRY OF HEALTH EVACUATION SCHEME

I asked Grandad about his lessons.

He said,

'We mostly learned
the three Rs — reading,
writing and arithmetic.'

Reading book

Maths book

'We also learned
geography and history.'

'We didn't do gym or PE.
We did stretching exercises,
called drill, outside.'

'The school had a garden.
We helped to grow vegetables.
There was a shortage of food
because of the war.'

I asked Grandad what he remembers most about his school days.

He said,

'The best lessons were nature walks.
Sometimes, we went down to the stream
and caught sticklebacks.
We put them in an aquarium
on the windowsill.'

'There were two playgrounds —
one for boys and one for girls.
We spent a lot of time playing marbles.'

'At playtime, we had
little bottles of milk
with cardboard tops.
In winter,
the milk froze.'

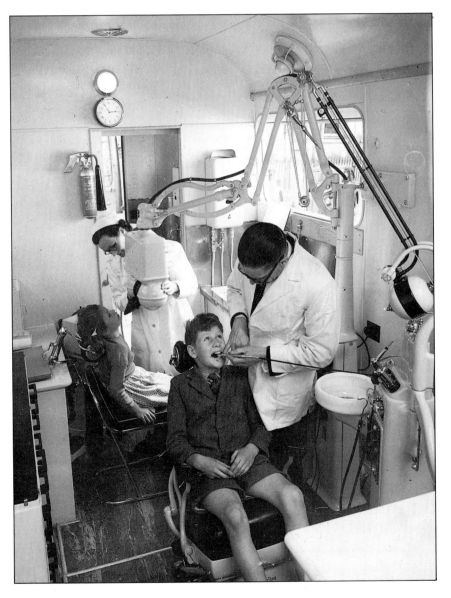

'Once a year, a caravan appeared
in the playground.
It was the dentist.
One time, he pulled two of my teeth out.'

Great-grandad went to the same school
from the age of 5 until he left at the age of 14.

He said,

'We didn't wear a uniform.
Boys wore knickerbockers
and shirts with stiff collars.
Girls wore dresses, often
with a white pinafore on top.'

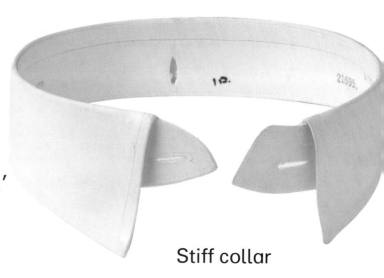

Stiff collar

'We sat at desks in rows.
We had to sit up straight.
The teacher stood at the front
of the class by the blackboard.'

'Everyone learned to read together.
The teacher pointed
to a word on the blackboard
and we all read it out.'

'When we could read,
we took turns to read aloud
a few sentences each
from a reading book.'

23

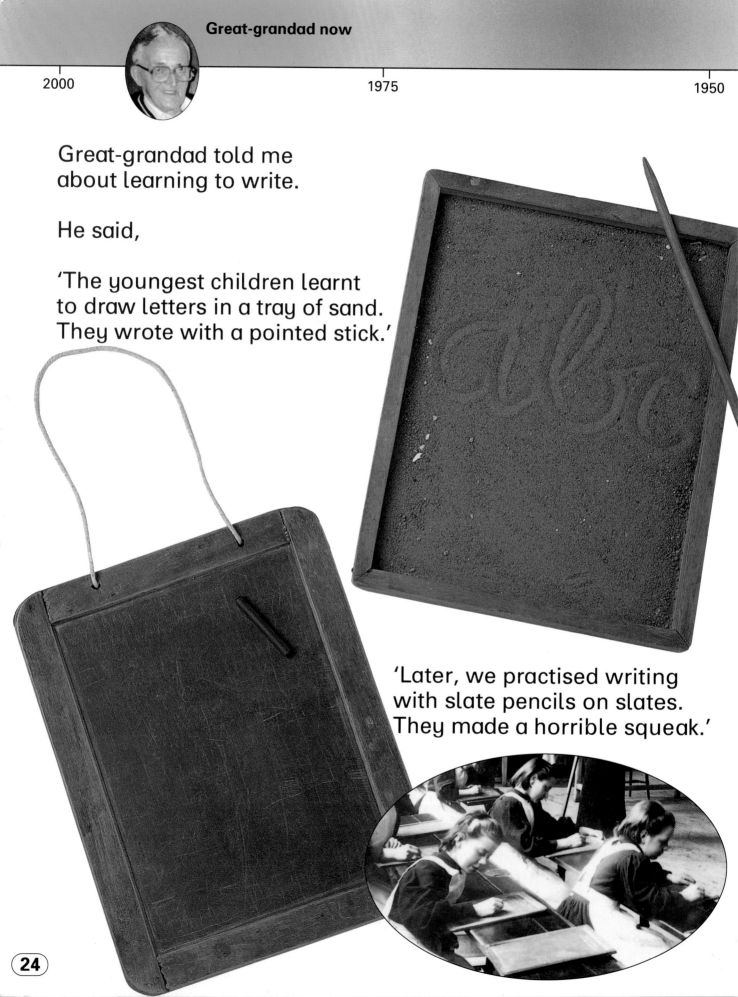

Great-grandad told me
about learning to write.

He said,

'The youngest children learnt
to draw letters in a tray of sand.
They wrote with a pointed stick.'

'Later, we practised writing
with slate pencils on slates.
They made a horrible squeak.'

Ink

'When we were older,
we wrote with pen and ink.
We had inkwells in our desks.
We dipped the pens into the ink.'

Ink jug for
filling inkwells

Dip pen

Inkwell

'We wrote in a copy book.
We copied out the printed writing
four times, as neatly as we could.'

I asked Great-grandad
what else he did at school.

He said,

'We learned about kings and queens
and other countries.'

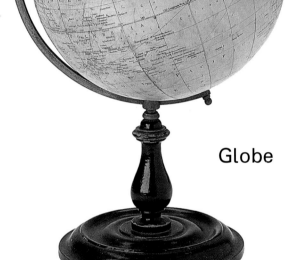

Globe

'We went on nature walks
and painted flowers and insects.'

'We had
drawing lessons.
Sometimes,
we copied patterns
on drawing cards.'

1925

1900

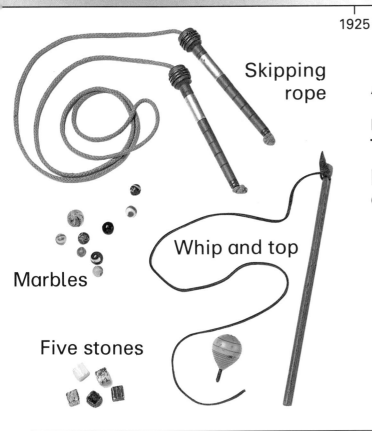

Skipping
rope

Marbles

Whip and top

Five stones

'At playtime, we played
marbles or five stones.
The girls skipped or
played with hoops
or whips and tops.'

Hoop

'When I was old enough, I played
in my school football team.'

I asked Great-grandad what he remembers
most about school.

He said,

'The teachers were very strict.
If you misbehaved, you were sent
to the headmaster.
He caned you on the hand.'

'One of the best things was Empire Day.
We dressed up and had a parade
through the village.'

28

'At the end of the year, there was a prize-giving.'

'Children got
certificates for
good work.'

'Sometimes,
we were given
books as prizes.'

'I was once given a medal
for not missing
a single day's school
all year.'

Things to do

In Great-grandad's time,
girls and boys had some lessons separately.
Girls learnt to cook, wash laundry and sew.
Boys had woodwork lessons.

Find out if your parents
or grandparents
had any separate lessons.
Do boys and girls
in your class have
any separate lessons?

Miniature clothes
made in sewing lessons

Dumb-bells

Show these pictures to different grown-ups.
Find out if they used any of these objects at school.
What were the objects used for?

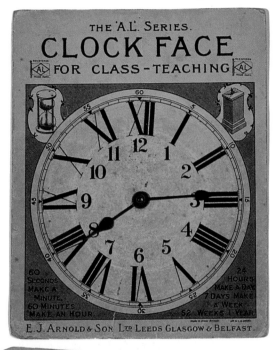

Clock face

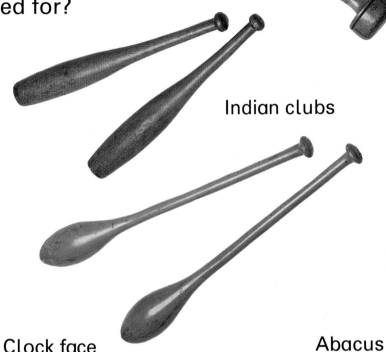

Indian clubs

Abacus

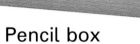

Pencil box

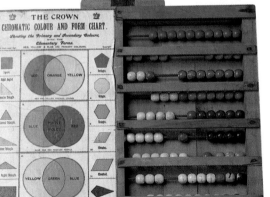

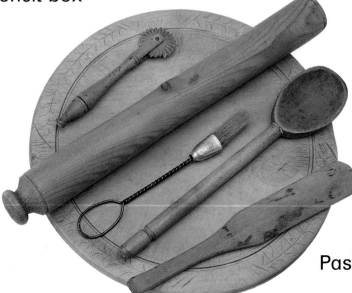

Pastry tools

Index